Draw Your Own Comic

This book belongs to

_____

ISBN-13 978-1719427227

ISBN-10 1719427224

DRAW YOUR OWN COMIC!

WRITING WORKBOOK &
BLANK COMIC BOOK

CONTENTS

Create Your Graphic Novel

Two award-winning authors have created this workbook show you, step by step, how to come up with an exciting story for your graphic novel. Whether you're making a comic, storyboarding a movie, brainstorming a novel, or creating manga, this workbook will help you produce a great adventure.

Many people start a graphic novel by drawing, but soon run out of ideas, or find their story isn't working.

By using this workbook, you will:

- Avoid common mistakes

- Create awesome characters

- Build a distinctive world for your story

- Create a plot with twists

- Explore professional writing techniques in an easy-to-use format

- Have fun drawing

So, let's get started.

Brainstorming Tips

- You can write, draw, mind map or scribble. This is your book, so do what suits you!

- Anything goes.

- Put down everything you think of, even the ideas that suck.

- The more ideas you jot down, the more your ideas will flow, and the more you'll have to choose from later.

- Don't worry about structure or ordering your ideas yet—that comes later.

- Go on, attack those brainstorming pages with confidence!

Creating Heroes and Villains

At the heart of every story is a hero who won't give up, no matter what. Evil villains and dangerous situations must push your hero to breaking point.

Your heroes and villains will drive your story. Their goals, their powers and their flaws will determine a lot of the action.

Readers love characters they can relate to. Heroes who are not perfect, who care about something important, and have fears, but are still courageous. Villains should also have goals, fears, strengths and personality.

Everyone loves to hate a memorable villain!

The following pages will help you develop your characters.

Superhero

Draw your Superhero

About

Super Powers

Flaws

Gadgets & Equipment

Draw your Supervillain

About

Super Powers

- laser vision
- speed
- fire webs

Flaws

Gadgets & Equipment

Hero

Draw your Hero

SuperPowers

Flaws

Equipment

About

Villain

Draw your Villain

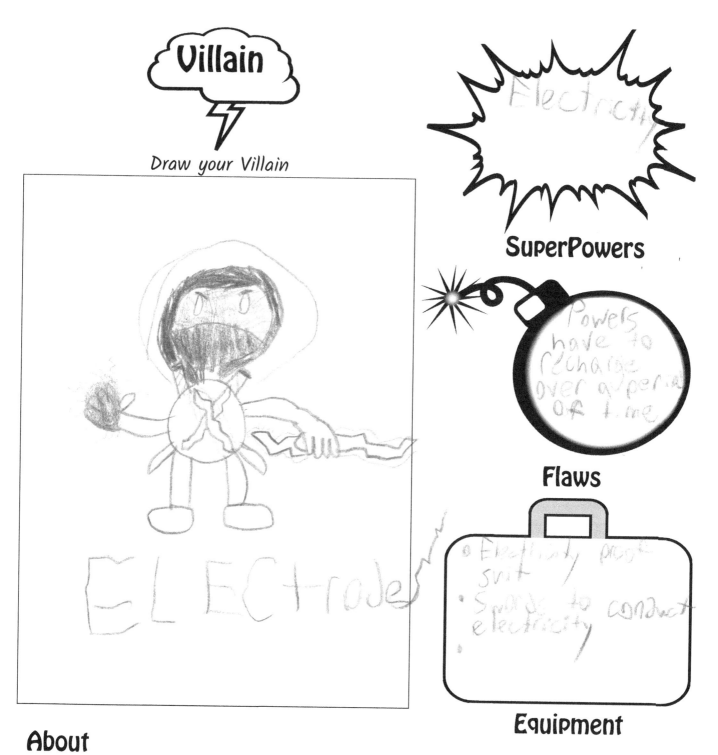

SuperPowers

Electricity

Flaws

Powers have to recharge over a period of time

Equipment

- Electricity proof suit
- Sponge to conduct electricity

ELECTrode

About

Hero

Draw your Hero

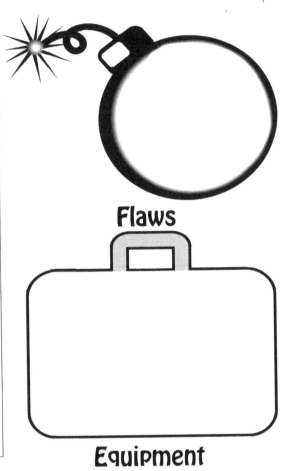

SuperPowers

Flaws

Equipment

About:

Draw your Villain

SuperPowers

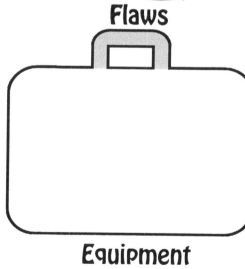

Flaws

Equipment

About:

Your World

Determining your setting is called **world building**.

Where does your story take place? Is it on Earth, another planet or at a Japanese school for ninjas? Your world will shape your characters, your plot and the flavor of your story.

We'll start with some basics, and then we'll look at how to handle magic when you're world building.

World name _____

World location (what universe, planet, country or city etc?) _____

_____

Interesting features (landscape, alien cities, magic forest, natural laws e.g. gravity or not?) _____

_____

_____

Problems in your world (scarce resources e.g. food, fuel etc; corrupt law-keepers; pollution;

alien forces attacking; war; plague; powerful magic users) _____

_____

_____

Your favorite things about this world _____

_____

_____

_____

Brainstorm Your World

Magic Rules

Every world or setting has limitations. If your world has magic or magical superpowers, then you need to decide where the powers come from, and if these powers come with a cost.

Magic rule examples

- Supergirl's and Superman's magic comes from the yellow sun, but they lose all their strength around Kryptonite. They also have no powers on a planet without a yellow sun.

- Batman can use the tools on his utility belt or Batmobile, but these things don't help him when he's Bruce Wayne—although his money and influence do!

The source of your magic

Where does the magic in your world draw its power from? Does it come from the user? Or from the environment? Does using magic make your hero tired? Do the villains have control of the superhero's power source?

Magic limitations

Your magic needs limits or your hero's job will be too easy.

Magic should be consistent throughout your story. You can't change the rules half way through the story. You can't do advanced magic at Hogwarts until you learn the spells. You can't swim in a library. And even Superman has to keep his identity secret.

Perhaps your characters can only fly when it's dark? Maybe magic comes from a well that's running dry. Perhaps magical creatures are threatened when you overuse magic, because you're using their life force.

What magic do you want in your world?

Brainstorm Your Magic Rules

Color scheme

Your color scheme will influence the flavor of your world and your story. Colors also change how people feel about characters and events. Before you start drawing, think about whether you want bright, funky or dark settings. E.g. Gloomy cellars, colorful furniture, shiny rocket ships or sparkling rainbows. This may change throughout your story depending on the mood and locations.

Think about how your characters will look in your settings e.g. do you have bright characters against a dark background? Is your hero's hangout all pink?

A character might blush or turn green with envy, but there are other ways to show the reader how the character feels - bright sunshine, storm clouds, blue skies, or dim lighting.

Experimenting with color

- What is your color palette?
  - Gritty and dark?
  - Bright and friendly?
  - Earthy or modern?
- How do your characters and settings fit your color?
- What colors will you use for high conflict, anger, crisis or triumph?
- When do you want your colors to clash, and when should they harmonize?

Use the opposite page to play with color.

Once you're happy with your color scheme, you can try it out on the following pages: *Superhero Hangout, Hero's Hangouts, Villain's Lair, Other Hangouts,* and *Draw Your World.*

Experiment with Color

Superhero Hangout

Hero's Hangouts

Villain's Lair

Other Hangouts

Draw Your World

Plotting, Planning & Scheming
What's a plot?

A plot is a summary of the main events in your story.

You don't have to plan a story. You can just start. However, writing down your ideas helps you keep on track with your story. If you don't, you may get lost chasing new ideas down dead-end alleys.

Making your story exciting

We've all seen movies that have us on the edge of our seats, biting our nails, hoping the hero will win against impossible odds.

Every good story has conflict at its core. It's this conflict that creates tension and hooks the readers. If you give us characters we care about, with an important cause, we'll want to know what happens to them.

What are your favorite stories?   Why do you like them?

Coming up with great ideas

Before you start a story, it's a good idea to brainstorm truckloads of ideas, so you can choose the best ones. Your heroes need problems to solve. Problems big enough to matter. Problems that will keep our readers hooked and turning the page.

The next two pages are blank so you can brainstorm. Use these questions to help you create cool problems for your heroes and villains and plot the main events in your story.

1. What does your main hero want most in the world?
2. What is stopping the hero from getting it?
3. What terrible things will happen if your heroes don't get what they want?
4. Who will suffer? What will be lost?
5. What does your villain want most in the world?
6. What stops the villain from getting it?
7. What will happen if the villain gets their own way?
8. Who will suffer?
9. What is the main problem your hero faces?
10. What weaknesses does the hero have that stop them from solving that problem?
11. How can you make this problem worse?
12. Is there a time-bomb ticking? A short amount of time to save the day?

The more problems your heroes face, the more interesting your story will be.

Brainstorm Your Story's Plot

Your Plot

Hopefully, you have lots of good ideas on your brainstorming page. If you haven't come up with many ideas, you could:

- Talk to a friend about your ideas.

- Think about your favorite books and movies to see what other writers do.

- Take a break, and try again after some exercise. Brains often come up with great ideas when you pretend you're not working!

Here's an easy formula for an exciting plot:

1. Start with your hero's main problem.

2. Make this problem get worse as the story goes on. Sometimes the hero makes things worse, even when they're trying to save the day. Sometimes it's the villain's fault.

3. Add another complication.

4. Right when we least expect it, the hero finally saves the day.

Now it's time to turn our ideas into an evil plot.

mwah, ha ha ha!

1. Our hero's biggest problem. →	Aquagirl must save the whales in their Pacific Ocean hunting grounds from whalers.

2. Complication: How does the hero (or villain) make the problem worse? →	Aquagirl disables the whaler's harpoons, but the whalers refuse to leave. They run ashore on the rocks and create an oil spill.

3. Added complication: How does the problem get worse again? What happens? →	Aquagirl uses wool to clean the spill, but while she's busy, the whalers have found a new harpoon and start killing whales.

4. Our hero saves the day! →	Aquagirl and the whales swim in circles, creating a whirlpool to funnel the remaining oil into an underground cavern. The oil is sucked down, but so is the harpoon. Squealing, the whalers fall into the freezing-cold ocean. Aquagirl has to seal the cavern with wool - and convince the whales to rescue the whalers. Grudglingly, the whales agree. The whalers are so happy to be alive, they form the Whale Protection League.

Design Your Plot

Now's the exciting part. You get to fill in your plot!

1. Establish your hero's main problem.

2. Introduce exciting twists and turns in your story, by making the hero's problem worse.

   As life gets more difficult for your hero, your readers will be cheering them on while biting their nails.

3. Make the hero's problems worse again.

   Now, your awesome readers will be biting their knuckles! And hoping the hero will succeed against all odds!

4. Don't worry about the ending yet. You'll be exploring great endings over the page.

Hints:

- Use your brainstorming page and highlight the ideas you like best.

- Choose different colors for each stage of the plot.

- Don't be afraid to add new ideas, or throw out ones that aren't working with the rest of the story.

- There's a full plot plan on page 47, with all four steps, so don't worry if this one gets messy!

Your hero's biggest problem:

↓

Complication:

↓

Added complication:

↓

Hero saves the day: (Don't worry about this yet, we'll cover it soon!)

The Ultimate Twist—Your Unexpected Ending

It's great when your ending surprises the reader. But how can we create a twist or unexpected ending?

Your ending can be humorous or dramatic, but it should have meaning. Readers like to see heroes triumph, people saved or a disaster averted. They don't usually like stories where they can see the ending coming, or where everybody dies. One ending is too obvious and the other is unsatisfying. If a reader is investing their time, we need to reward them.

Writers make their heroes clever by hiding clues in the story. These clues often get forgotten...but then, the hero uses them in an unexpected way, saving everyone!

As a writer, you get to decide what your twist is. Don't worry if your ideas are any good or not. Brainstorming bad endings and obvious ones will help you have other ideas about what could work.

1. What are three obvious ways your hero could solve the problem?

2. What are the three worst endings you could think of?

3. What are the three ways your hero could use their flaw to save the day?

4. Is there any equipment the hero could use? How?

5. Does the villain have a flaw that your hero could take advantage of?

6. Is there an unexpected way the hero could use their powers?

7. Can your heroes team together to save the day? How?

8. Can the hero team with a minor character?

9. Is there something about your world (magic, place etc.) that could make a difference?

10. What other ideas do you have? Check your brainstorming, world & character pages.

Brainstorming Your Twist

Final Plot

Your hero's biggest problem:

Complication:

Added complication:

Hero saves the day:

Your Elevator Pitch

Authors never know when they'll meet a publisher in an elevator, so they prepare an elevator pitch – a couple of snappy sentences that will sell their book. You may not meet a publisher, but you may want to tell your friends about your story.

The back cover blurb of Rick Riordon's *The Lightning Thief* is a great elevator pitch:

> *Percy Jackson is about to be kicked out of boarding school...again. And that's the least of his troubles. Lately, mythological monsters and the gods of Mount Olympus seem to be walking straight out of the pages of Percy's Greek mythology textbook and into his life.*

Did you notice the structure? A hero faces a problem that gets worse.

- Hero: *Percy Jackson*

- Problem: *about to be kicked out of boarding school*

- Complication: *mythological monsters and the gods of Mount Olympus*

An elevator pitch is just for fun. If you'd like to try and write one, look at your plot for your hero, problem, and complication.

Hero

Problem

Complication

Your Elevator Pitch

Dialogue & Thoughts

Speech

In comics and graphic novels, we write what characters say inside speech bubbles, which usually have smooth edges. The tail of the bubble points towards the person speaking.

Wow, I can hear myself talking. Thank you!

Thoughts

Your character's thoughts are written inside fluffy bubbles that look like clouds. Puffy bubbles float from the person's head up to the thought cloud.

Unless you have characters with super mind-reading powers, only the character with the thought cloud knows what they are thinking.

Mwah ha ha ha. No one knows my evil thoughts.

Subtext

Subtext is a cool technique that writers use to show characters saying one thing, but thinking something different.

Drawing & Design Tips

Before you start drawing, here are a few tips:

- Draw lightly in pencil, so you can make changes if you want

- When you're finished, you can go over your pictures with ink

- Make sure your characters are looking at each other so the pictures feel realistic

- To make sure you have enough space for speech and thoughts in your story, it's easiest to

  o   write the dialogue (words) first

  o   then draw speech bubbles (or thought bubbles) around the words

  o   then draw the characters

  o   then draw the background

- Words in graphic novels are usually all CAPITALS, but you can choose your own style

- You can **BOLD** words to make them stronger, or make words LARGER when characters yell

- If your heroes or villains move to a new hangout or setting, show your readers some detail of the location before you draw a close-up scene.

If you need more graphic novels for another project, we have many styles, including blank graphic novels and comics.

CREATE A COMIC

Let's Get Drawing!

You've built an amazing world

You've created cool heroes and villainous villains

Your magic is ready to rock

Your hangouts are waiting

Your plots are twisted

& Your twists are plotted

You're ready to start drawing!

The opposite blank page is for your cover design

Then turn the page and go for it.

4

8

14

17

18

41

44

45

If you need more graphic novels for another project, we have many styles, including blank graphic novels and comics.

CREATE A COMIC

Made in the USA
Middletown, DE
24 October 2021